SPANISH CIVIL WAR

A History From Beginning to End

Copyright © 2018 by Hourly History.

D1411518

Table of Contents

Introduction

For most Spanish people, their civil war was the defining event of the twentieth century. Spain took no direct part in the First or Second World Wars or in any of the South-East Asian wars which followed. For most Spanish, their civil war is known simply as "the War."

Still, the Spanish Civil War is one of the least known and documented wars, in part because Spain seems determined to repress its memory. Although the war left an indelible scar on the Spanish psyche, an agreement to ignore it was signed into law in 1977, known as the Pact of Forgetting (*el pacto del olvido*). The history of the civil war is generally not taught in Spanish schools, there are almost no public memorials to those killed, and recent attempts by forensic pathologists to uncover the graves of those murdered during the conflict have been met with apathy and on occasion outright opposition.

This is not a simple war to understand. The causes seem complex to outsiders, the fighting often involved a number of small factions working virtually independently, and outside intervention wasn't just important, it defined much of the course of the war. However, the Spanish Civil War is important not only for itself but because, in retrospect, it prefigured much of what was to follow in World War II. The first time that German and Russian tanks, aircraft, and soldiers fought each other wasn't when Germany invaded Russia in 1941, it was on and over the battlefields of Spain. Improvements in military technology and the strategy and tactics of modern war were refined during the civil war. The German Blitzkrieg which would devastate Europe a few years later was first rehearsed during this war.

The Spanish Civil War is often seen as a laboratory where powerful nations began to perfect the hardware and tactics that they would later use in a global war. But it was much more than this; the civil war was a baffling, internecine conflict fought between people who often weren't entirely clear about what or who they were fighting for or against.

Chapter One

Into the Abyss

"We do not believe in government through the voting booth."

—Francisco Franco

In the sixteenth and seventeenth centuries, Spain was the most powerful nation on earth and supported by one of the largest empires ever seen. Treasures from South America flowed into Spain at an unprecedented rate and provided staggering wealth for a small number of people. By the early 1800s, this wealth and the military power it had purchased was almost gone. At the Battle of Trafalgar in 1805, the Spanish fleet was destroyed, leaving Spain with no means of protecting the remnants of its empire. In 1808, French forces under the command of Napoleon invaded Spain and Portugal, bringing destruction and death to the Iberian Peninsula.

One hundred years later, Spain was a poor and mainly agrarian country ruled by a constitutional monarchy under King Alfonso XIII. Corruption was endemic at all levels of government and made even worse by inefficiency and incompetence amongst officials who had often purchased their positions. The Catholic Church occupied a vital and influential role in Spanish society. In 1921, there was a rebellion in one of the few overseas possessions still controlled by Spain: Spanish Morocco. An army was sent to quash the rebellion. Instead, it was massacred by local tribesmen leading to wide-scale protests and demonstrations. In 1923, King Alfonso agreed that General Primo de Rivera should take charge of the country in order to quell unrest and re-establish the rule of law.

Although he ruled as a military dictator, Rivera proved adept at managing the Spanish economy, and under his control unemployment fell and industrial output increased hugely. In 1925, Rivera was even able to bring Morocco back under Spanish control. However, the worldwide recession of the late 1920s hit Spain hard. Rivera was not able to solve the subsequent financial problems, and he resigned in late 1930, prompting a general election.

The elections in April 1931 brought to power the Republicans, a coalition of left-wing parties who wanted to create a new Spanish Republic (Spain had briefly been a republic in 1873, for less than one year). The ruling group, which became known as the Popular Front, included both socialists and communists and quickly abolished the monarchy and announced the start of the Second Spanish Republic.

The members of the coalition which made up the Popular Front were also opposed to the Catholic Church, which they saw as having too great an influence on Spanish society. This aspect of their policies was particularly abhorrent to people in the middle and upper classes who saw the Church as an important element of stability and conservatism in Spain.

The Popular Front was far from a unified group. It included the right-wing of the Spanish Socialist Party but was opposed by the left wing of the same party which wanted revolution rather than gradual change. It also included the powerful Spanish Communist Party, but in parliament it was opposed by the influential anarchist group the Confederación Nacional del Trabajo (CNT) who were committed to the overthrow of capitalism and to socialist revolution as well as to Basque and Catalan separation. Chaos and confrontation followed the elections, and in 1933, the collapse of the Popular Front government prompted new elections in which the extreme right swept to power.

The new ruling group comprised industrialists, monarchists, and admirers of the fascist successes of Adolf Hitler in Germany and Benito Mussolini in Italy. Over the next three years, the country was almost crippled by a series of strikes and violent confrontations as supporters of the Popular Front opposed the new ruling group. In early 1936, new elections were called. The extreme left once more swept to power, but the new Popular Front government was so divided by internal squabbles that it failed to establish control over the country. Spain descended once more into chaos and anarchy.

In May 1936, the relatively conservative President Niceto Zamora was replaced by the radical Manuel Azaña, and Spain lurched even further to the left. As a direct reaction to this development, a group of senior army officers which included General José Sanjurjo and General Emilio Mola began to discuss the possibility of a coup to overthrow the Popular Front government. They also spoke with the governor of the Canary Islands, General Francisco Franco, a military commander whose ruthlessness had enraged the Popular Front when he had sent troops against strikers in Catalonia. Many supporters of the right began to wonder whether a military dictatorship might be the solution to Spain's continuing political problems and whether Generals Franco, Mola, and Sanjurjo might be the people best placed to lead it.

Events were precipitated on July 12, 1936 in Madrid when members of a right-wing fascist Falange group murdered José Castillo, an officer in the elite Republican paramilitary group called the Assault Guard. Members of the Assault Guard responded with violence which included the murder of José Calvo Sotelo, a politician of the extreme right, on July 13. On July 19, General Mola issued a proclamation in the northern city of Navarre calling for a revolt against the Popular Front government. General Franco made a radio appeal asking all army officers to join the revolt. By the end of July 1936, rebel Nationalist forces under the command of the generals were in combat with Republican forces directed by the Popular Front. The Spanish Civil War had begun.

Chapter Two

Taking Positions

"One Country! One State! One Chief! Franco! Franco! Franco!"

—Nationalist Civil War Poster

The generals who led the Nationalist revolt had hoped that large numbers of Spanish people would immediately join them when the proclamation of revolt was issued in Navarre, but the response was initially disappointing. Only in Seville in the south and Aragón in the north of Spain were there anything more than isolated pockets of Nationalist insurrection. The revolt suffered a further blow when General José Sanjurjo was killed in an aircraft crash on the day after the issuing of the proclamation, leaving Mola and Franco as the principal leaders of the rebellion. There were suspicions—though these were never confirmed—that Franco had Sanjurjo killed to ensure that he would be able to take control of the Nationalists. These suspicions would only deepen when General Mola also died in an air crash, leaving Franco in sole command of all Nationalist forces.

Following the proclamation by General Mola, President Azaña initially attempted to negotiate with the Nationalist rebels, but it became apparent that they were not interested in any form of compromise. Instead, Prime Minister José Giral decided to try to protect the Popular Front government by distributing weapons to a number of left-wing organizations. The plan was that these were to be used to contain and eventually destroy the rebel enclaves in Spain.

The Spanish Army was completely split by the rebellion. The Peninsular Army (the portion of the army permanently based in mainland Spain) had around 9,000 officers and 100,000 men in the summer of 1936. When General Mola issued his proclamation, around half the officers of the Peninsular Army immediately joined the Nationalist forces while around 2,000 joined the Republican forces defending the Popular Front. Roughly half the men joined the Nationalists while the rest joined the Republicans. The Army of Africa based in Morocco joined the Nationalist side under the command of General Franco and formed the first wave of Nationalist troops to be airlifted and transferred by ship to southern Spain.

By the summer of 1936, rebel Nationalist forces held just two areas of Spain. In the south, they had around 60,000 men under the command of General Franco and controlled areas around the port of Ferrol in addition to the cities of Huelva, Cadiz, Cordoba, Granada, and Seville. In the north, they had around 100,000 men under the command of General Mola and controlled a large area including the provinces of Galicia, León, Navarre, and parts of Old Castile and Aragón. The rest of the country—including the capital Madrid and other major cities such as Barcelona and Valencia—was under the control of the

150,000 men who comprised the Republican forces loyal to the Popular Front government. But the Republican army was not a homogenous force; it was made up of a number of separate groups including communist, anarchist, and socialist militias.

The Nationalists also received support, supplies, and equipment from Portugal. The authoritarian government of Portugal under the control of President Antonio Salazar feared the spread of left-wing politics to their country because a Portuguese version of the Popular Front was gaining support. President Salazar immediately had supporters of this group arrested and closed the Spanish-Portuguese frontier to Republicans while continuing to ship military equipment and supplies to Nationalist forces in Spain.

The Nationalists were initially at a military disadvantage because, in the early stages of the war, their forces were physically divided into two main regions in the north and the south. In the south, they were also confined to a number of small pockets around major cities. However, from the outset, Republican forces were hampered by major political and ideological differences between different armed factions. The president and leader of the Popular Front, Manuel Azaña, was a socialist, but his government had never received the support of the largest anarchist party in Spain, the Confederación Nacional del Trabajo (CNT), which was particularly powerful in Barcelona where it supported the cause of Catalan separatists. Initially, the CNT refused to support the Popular Front, and it wasn't until November

1936 that the anarchists finally agreed to send four members to join the cabinet (including feminist journalist Federica Montseny who became Health Minister and the first ever female member of a cabinet in Spain). Still, the relationship between the anarchists and the Popular Front was always an uneasy one, especially because there was a deep and lasting historical antipathy between the CNT and the Spanish Communist Party (PCE) which was also an important part of the Popular Front coalition.

The Popular Front was also supported by the Workers Party of Marxist Unification (POUM), a revolutionary communist but anti-Stalinist party which supported the teachings of Leon Trotsky. The POUM was based in Catalonia and had formed an uneasy truce with the CNT but was viewed with great suspicion by the pro-Stalin PCE. Each of these groups—the PCE, POUM, and CNT—had their own armed militia units which were fighting the Nationalists independently of the main army of the government.

The left-wing Republican armed forces were initially hampered by an attempt to bring socialism to the activities of its army. All military ranks were abolished (all members of the Republican armed forces were to be addressed only as *comrade*), and military command was undertaken by elected soldiers' councils rather than by orders issued by officers. This was a bold experiment, but it quickly became clear that referring to councils for decisions was inappropriate in a modern war—some Republican units were overrun during early fighting as they waited for their councils to debate and decide what to do next.

Towards the end of 1936, a new prime minister of the Popular Front was appointed, Largo Caballero. One of his first actions was to re-establish military ranks and a chain of command and to abolish the soldiers' councils. This helped to make Republican armed forces more effective though it also alienated many left-wing supporters as well as the newly amalgamated anarchists.

While the Republicans struggled with internal divisions, General Franco strengthened his position as leader of the Nationalists. In September 1936, he was declared both Spanish Chief of State and commander of all Nationalist forces; General Mola agreed to serve under him and became Commander of the Army of the North. Franco proved just as ruthless in dealing with allies who he saw as potential rivals as he was in attacking the Republicans. Many senior leaders of the Nationalist movement who Franco didn't consider sufficiently loyal were removed from command and sent into exile. Franco made no attempt to rescue the former military dictator of Spain, General Primo de Rivera, from Republican captivity, even though he knew that it was very likely that de Rivera would be executed. Franco feared that if de Rivera joined the Nationalist Army, he would become a rival. Franco was therefore probably not too distraught when de Rivera was finally shot by his Republican captors in November 1936, though he wasted no time in cranking up the Nationalist propaganda machine to venerate de Rivera as a martyr to the Nationalist cause.

For the remainder of the civil war, Franco would remain in sole and undisputed control of all Nationalist military forces. Within six months of becoming Chief of State, he also forced the merging of all Spanish right-wing parties into one new political group: the Falange Española Tradicionalista with himself as the leader. It wasn't long before posters began to appear all over Nationalist-held areas showing the face of Franco and bearing the slogan: "One Country! One State! One Chief!"

Like Adolf Hitler in Germany and Benito Mussolini in Italy, Franco intended to make himself the absolute military and political leader of Spain. Franco's ruthless accumulation of political and military power had the advantage of ensuring that Nationalist forces pursued a single policy while the Republicans would struggle with factionalism and ideological differences throughout the civil war.

Chapter Three

Opening Moves

"You don't fight a war with words, but with fortifications."

—Buenaventura Durruti

The first objective for Nationalist forces was the capture of the Spanish capital: Madrid. By November 1, 1936, 25,000 Nationalist troops under the command of General Jose Varela were in the outskirts of the city where they encountered strong resistance from Republican forces. Both sides recognized the importance of occupying Madrid, and the battles for control of that city were to become the most bitter and protracted of the whole civil war.

On the November 6, Prime Minister Largo Caballero decided that it would be wise if he and the Popular Front government left the city. The government relocated to Valencia, an act that was seen as cowardice and betrayal by many Republicans who believed that the government should have remained in the besieged city. Before leaving, Caballero gave instructions that Madrid was to be held at all costs. The defense of Madrid was to last for three years and would give rise to one of the most famous slogans of the civil war: "*¡No pasarán!*" ("They shall not pass!"). The slogan was first used in a speech by Dolores Gómez, a

Spanish communist. When the city was finally taken by Nationalist forces in March 1939, General Franco muttered "*Hemos pasado*" ("We passed").

The first attack on Madrid was also the first major battle of the civil war. Repeated attacks by Nationalist forces in November and December 1936 led to around 15,000 casualties for the attackers and a similar number for the defending Republicans. As the Nationalists rushed additional troops to bolster the attack, the Republicans brought in more troops from other parts of Spain to defend. On November 14, the Anarchist Brigade arrived from Aragon, under the command of its charismatic leader Buenaventura Durruti. This was the first time that communist, socialist, and anarchist troops of the Popular Front had fought together, but there was a high degree of distrust between the different factions of Republicans. The unease was made worse when, just one week after his arrival, Durruti was killed. It was announced that he had been shot by a Nationalist sniper, but many anarchists believed that he had been murdered by the communists.

The attacks on Madrid continued throughout the winter and spring of 1937 and caused a large number of casualties on both sides. The Republican defenders were able to retain possession of the city, and the Nationalists began to look for other ways in which they could expand the territory they held. At the beginning of 1937, Republicans held a strip of the coast of southern Spain centered around Malaga, the main base for the Republican Navy. In mid-January, Nationalist forces attacked this area to the east from Cadiz and Seville and to the west from Granada. In February, they took control of the city of Malaga.

Also in February 1937, Nationalists began attempts to cut Madrid off from the rest of Republican-controlled Spain. In February, Nationalist troops attacked over the river Jarama in an effort to cut the road between Madrid and Valencia. The ensuing battle was indecisive; the road remained open, but both sides suffered casualties of around 10,000 each. Then over 50,000 Nationalist troops attacked the town of Guadalajara, 60 kilometers northwest of Madrid, on March 8 in a further attempt to encircle the city. After a Republican counter-attack, the Nationalist were driven back with both sides once again suffering heavy casualties.

In May and again in July, Republican forces in Madrid made concerted efforts to break out from encircling Nationalist forces. Neither of these battles achieved anything other than inflicting heavy casualties on both sides. Madrid remained under siege for the remainder of the war, but there would never again be a major battle for control of the city.

In early May 1937, suspicion and distrust between different groups within the Republicans led to factional fighting in the city of Barcelona. Members of the Communist Party (PCE) were pushing to be given a more important role in government, something that Prime Minister Caballero consistently refused to do. Consequently, Caballero was replaced by Juan Negrín who promptly appointed members of the PCE to many of the main civilian and military posts.

On May 3, police attempted to take control of the telephone exchange in Barcelona which was under the control of armed supporters of the CNT. They failed, and the CNT and POUM built barricades in the city where they began fighting with police and members of the PCE the following day. On May 6, a number of prominent anarchists were assassinated, and on May 7, over 6,000 Republican Guards from Valencia attacked the city. More than 400 people died in the riots that followed before order could be restored.

At a time when the Republican cause was fighting for its very survival against the Nationalists, factions within it seemed more concerned with limiting the power of other groups than with fighting the common enemy.

Chapter Four

Outside Intervention—The Nationalists

"The Spanish Civil War gave me an opportunity to put my young air force to the test, and a means for my men to gain experience."

—Herman Goering, head of the Luftwaffe

One of the most notable and unusual aspects of the Spanish Civil War was the level of foreign participation—a large proportion of the combatants on each side were not Spanish, and much of the military hardware used originated from other countries. In part, this reflected the rise in Europe of two opposing ideologies: fascism and communism. The war in Spain became an extension of the political conflict between these two opposing views into a military confrontation. Some of the countries who would later become involved in World War II also used the conflict in Spain as a way to train soldiers and to refine strategies, tactics, and equipment which would be used in the later war.

Europe in the mid-1930s was a place of political turmoil. The economic crisis of the 1920s had left many people without savings and distrustful of the systems that had allowed these things to happen. People were looking to new types of politics which might, they hoped, bring security and a new sense of order.

During World War I, the existing political system in Russia had been overthrown by the Bolsheviks who put in its place a communist state ruled by a central committee. By the mid-1930s, the Soviet Union was wholly under the autocratic and sometimes brutal rule of General Secretary Joseph Stalin. Around the world, new communist parties emerged, encouraged by the successful revolution in Russia. The Soviet Union, under Stalin's guidance, provided money and, where appropriate, weapons and other equipment to allow these parties to establish communist regimes in their own countries.

In Italy, fascist leader and dictator Benito Mussolini had been in complete control of the country since 1925. Mussolini was very keen to demonstrate the might of the Italian armed forces without anything as drastic as a full-scale war, and he saw the conflict in Spain as a battle between fascist (Nationalist) and communist (Republican) forces. Mussolini was therefore enthusiastic about sending Italian troops to support the Nationalists in Spain. Fascism had also proved immensely popular in Germany where Adolf Hitler and the Nazi Party had been elected to power in 1933. Hitler foresaw a European war which he believed would involve Germany and France, and he regarded the prospect of having a friendly fascist power on France's western border as something that would benefit Germany. Hitler also therefore decided that he would support the Nationalist side in the conflict.

Britain and France were concerned about the prospect of other European countries being drawn into the conflict in Spain, and in September 1936, just as fighting was beginning to spread across Spain, both countries proposed a Non-Intervention Agreement. This pact was intended to ensure that there would be no outside intervention in the Spanish Civil War, and it was signed by 27 countries including Germany, Italy, and the Soviet Union.

But during the first three months of the civil war, while Italian politicians were signing the Non-Intervention Pact, Italy sent more than 90 military aircraft for use by the Nationalists and re-fitted the *Canarias*—the largest warship belonging to the Nationalists—in an Italian naval yard. In November, Italy signed a secret treaty with the Nationalists agreeing to supply tanks, aircraft, cannons, thousands of machine guns, and ammunition to the Nationalists. In return, Franco agreed that, in the event of a European war, Italy would be able to use bases in Spain.

In December, Mussolini began sending troops to Spain. Initially, these were volunteers who joined Black Shirt units of the Nationalist Army. By the end of 1936, Italy was also sending fully equipped Italian regular army units to fight under Franco. By the end of 1936, there were over 3,000 Italian fighters in the Nationalist Army; by March 1937, there were more than 50,000. When the Nationalists mounted the attack on Guadalajara with 50,000 men, 31,000 of those were Italian supported by

Italian aircraft, tanks, and machine guns and fighting under Italian officers.

During the course of the civil war, Italy sent over 80,000 men to Spain as well as a number of warships, hundreds of military aircraft, vehicles, and tanks, and thousands of cannon and machine guns. In 1937, Italian submarines began sinking Republican ships in the Mediterranean, though this prompted such international outrage that Mussolini was forced to call it off. Italy was the single largest source of outside troops and equipment during the civil war, and this intervention contributed to the Nationalist victory.

Nazi Germany also sent troops and equipment to support the Nationalist cause. The German intervention began almost as soon as the Nationalist rebellion was announced. General Franco needed transport aircraft to allow him to move large numbers of troops quickly from Morocco to the Spanish mainland. He asked Germany for help, and Adolf Hitler personally intervened to ensure that, in July 1936, 26 German fighters and 30 Junkers-52 transport aircraft were made available to the Nationalists to effect the rapid movement of troops from Morocco to mainland Spain.

Hitler sent a member of the German general staff, Lieutenant Colonel Walter Warlimont, to Spain to act as a military advisor to General Franco in September 1936. Warlimont advised Hitler that Franco needed additional military support if he was to win the war and suggested the formation of a German Condor Legion, which would comprise fighter and bomber aircraft with German pilots, aircrew, and ground staff. Hitler initially hesitated, but when the first attack on Madrid failed and it was discovered that the Republican defenders were being supported by Russian tanks and aircraft, Hitler agreed to the formation of a German military aviation group in Spain. His reasons weren't entirely altruistic—his aviation experts were also telling him that this was an excellent opportunity to test new German military aircraft as well as refining strategy and tactics. Initially, Hitler wanted to send only obsolete aircraft to Spain, but he was eventually persuaded to send the latest types so that they could be tested in combat conditions.

Over time, the Condor Legion would grow to include 12,000 men and operated as a virtually autonomous unit accountable only to General Franco himself. During the civil war, aircraft of the Condor Legion dropped almost 17 million kilos of bombs in Spain. The Condor Legion was supported on the ground by a much smaller German tank group. This group was never larger than 1,000 men and was generally used to train the Nationalists in the use of tanks. Just like the Condor Legion, the men of the German tank units in Spain were used to test and refine equipment and to improve German armored tactics.

Documents seized after the war suggest that Hitler also had another reason for allowing German military involvement—he wanted the civil war in Spain to drag-on as long as possible. Italian involvement in the war was high-profile, and Mussolini was continually attacked for his breaking of the Non-Intervention Agreement by the western powers and particularly by France and Britain.

This suited Hitler well as it drove Italy closer to Germany. In 1937, Italy joined the Anti-Comintern Pact, an anti-communist pact between Germany and Japan.

Germany used its involvement in Spain to develop and improve many of the tactics and weapons which would form part of the Blitzkrieg unleashed during World War II. For example, ground-air radio communication was improved to allow infantry units to call for dive-bomber support, fighter tactics were improved in light of combat experience in Spain, and Germany's main fighter, the Messerschmitt Bf 109, and its most important bomber, the Heinkel He 111, were both improved.

In addition to the support from Nazi Germany and fascist Italy, the Nationalist forces also received weapons, ammunition, and other supplies from President Salazar in neighboring Portugal. Without this massive external support, there is little doubt that the Nationalist rebellion would have quickly failed.

Chapter Five

Outside Intervention—The Republicans

"As Russian arms appeared and foreign volunteers gathered to serve in the Comintern-organized International Brigades, the poisonous tendrils of Stalinism began to smother Republican Spain."

—Piers Brendon, *The Dark Valley* (2000)

While Germany and Italy provided men and equipment for the Nationalist side, the Soviet Union provided the same for the Republicans. Just as Hitler and Mussolini saw the benefit of having another fascist country in Europe, Stalin was interested in the establishment of a new communist regime. Russia's involvement in the Spanish Civil War therefore took two distinct paths: First, the supply of aircraft, tanks, and other military equipment plus trained Russian operators to serve in Republican armed forces. Second, the elimination of non-communist elements within the Popular Front. Stalin's aim was not just a Republican victory, but a Republican Spain completely dominated by communists taking their orders direct from Moscow.

Stalin first approved Russian military intervention in September 1936, as details of Italian involvement on the Nationalist side began to be made public. By October, the first Russian warplanes and tanks were arriving in Spain, complete with pilots, crews, and trained support workers. The Russian Red Army Air Force supplied Polikarpov I-16 fighters (one of the most advanced fighters in the world at the time), and the Red Army provided large numbers of the T-26 tank, another advanced design which became the most important and numerous tank used in the civil war.

By the time of the Nationalist attack on Madrid at the end of 1936, the defenders were supported by large numbers of Russian I-16 fighters and T-26 tanks with Russian pilots and crews. Over the next nine months, the Soviet Union would supply the Republicans with one thousand aircraft, nine hundred tanks, and thousands of machine guns and artillery pieces. Up to one thousand Russian pilots and tank crews fought on the Republican side in Spain.

In addition to tanks and aircraft, Russia also sent to Spain agents of the People's Commissariat for Internal Affairs (NKVD). Although it was primarily a military police force, parts of the NKVD were similar to the German Gestapo and carried out secret police activities. In Spain, their mission was simple: they were to ensure that the Republican cause was dominated by the Spanish Communist Party (PCE) over which Russia exerted a great deal of control. The replacement of liberal Prime Minister Caballero with the communist sympathizer Juan Negrín in early 1937 quickly led to the appointment of

PCE members to vital roles in the cabinet. NKVD agents also carried out a number of arrests and executions of members of non-communist groups within the Popular Front including POUM, the CNT, and the FAI. The internal unrest caused by these killings substantially weakened the Republican cause, but Stalin seemed determined that a Republican victory in Spain must only be a communist victory.

In addition to sending equipment and Russian troops, Stalin also used the Communist International, an organization pledged to the worldwide spread of communism, to raise a number of International Brigades to fight on the Republican side in Spain. These brigades were made up of communist volunteers from France, Britain, America, and exiles from Nazi Germany and fascist Italy who wanted to fight against fascism in Spain. There were also several other non-communist volunteer units on the Republican side including elements of the POUM and CNT and anarcho-syndicalist units such as the Durruti Column.

By June 1937, the prospects for a Republican military victory were fading, and Stalin ordered that shipments of equipment to Spain should be drastically cut back. At this point, Soviet pilots and tank crews were also recalled to Russia. In 1938, the International Brigades were disbanded, and by the time that the civil war ended, there were very few foreign troops serving on the Republican side.

Stalin insisted that the Republicans pay for the support provided by Russia. Before the civil war began,

Spain had the fourth largest gold reserves in the world. Prime Minister Juan Negrín agreed that $500 million in gold (approximately three-quarters of the Spanish reserve) should be shipped to the Soviet Union to pay for tanks and aircraft in mid-1937.

It seems likely that without the tanks, aircraft, pilots, and crews supplied by Russia in the early stages of the war, the Republicans could not have stood against Nationalist armies which were supplied and supported by Germany and Italy. However, Russian support came at a very high cost, which did not only deplete Spanish gold reserves and was partly responsible for the wave of poverty which engulfed Spain in the years following the civil war, but it also brought internal conflict which ultimately weakened the Republican cause.

Chapter Six

The Terror

"We must extend the terror. We must impose the impression of dominion while eliminating without scruples everyone who does not think as we do."

—General Emilio Mola

All civil wars are brutal, but the Spanish Civil War was especially notable for the widespread killing of non-combatants, the execution of prisoners, and the deliberate employment of tactics designed to subdue opposition by the imposition of terror.

Massacres were almost routine during the civil war even from the very earliest days. When Nationalist troops occupied Malaga in early February 1937 for example, it has been estimated that around 4,000 suspected Republican sympathizers were summarily shot. Italian troops, who had been involved in the assault on the city, were reported to have been horrified by the scale and brutality of the killings of men and women. Some people—mainly pregnant women, women with young children, the elderly, and the sick—were spared execution but were instead driven out of the city to the east, on the N340 road towards Republican Almeria, 200 kilometers away. The thinking was, apparently, that this would force the Republicans to feed these refugees whereas if they had been allowed to remain in Malaga, it would have become the responsibility of the Nationalists.

It is estimated that up to 50,000 refugees fled Malaga on foot and began the long trek to Almeria. They were subjected to almost continual strafing by Nationalist aircraft, attacks by following Italian tanks, and shelling by German warships. There was no military justification for this; none of the people fleeing the city were combatants, and the harassment seems to have been done for no other reason than to terrorize the civilians. No one is certain how many people died en-route to Almeria. Estimates vary from three to five thousand. What is certain is that, even up to the 1980s, human remains were still being discovered next to the N340 which is now a major tourist route from Malaga to Almeria.

This deliberate brutality towards civilians and prisoners characterized much of the fighting during the civil war. When Nationalist forces first began their attacks on Madrid in late 1936, many prisoners held by the Republicans were shot. These included civilians, Catholic priests, and soldiers who were believed to be sympathetic towards the Nationalist cause. The numbers killed are uncertain, but estimates range from three to twelve thousand.

Other massacres involved killing by both sides. In and around the town of Badajoz, for example, many people suspected of being Nationalists were killed by Republicans almost as soon as the war began. At one point, in the town of Fuente de Cantos, 56 people were forced into a church by Republican soldiers. The church was then set on fire. When Nationalist troops took the province of Badajoz, up to 12,000 civilians were executed in reprisal. This pattern of massacre followed by reprisal massacre was repeated throughout the war.

In some cases, the killing of civilians was done as a kind of military experiment. The bombing of the town of Guernica was one of the most famous examples. In April 1937, it seems that Wolfram von Richthofen, cousin of the famous First World War fighter ace and a commander of the Condor Legion, was curious to see what the effect of bombing a small town would be in terms of civilian morale. The place chosen for this experiment was Guernica, a small market town in the Basque province of Biscay around 30 kilometers from Bilbao. Until April 1937, the town had not been directly affected by fighting during the civil war.

April 23 was market day in Guernica, and the town's usual population of around 5,000 people was swollen by large numbers of people attending the open-air market in the center of town. At around 16:30 in the afternoon, the first German aircraft dropped bombs over the town. For the next three hours, waves of German aircraft dropped an estimated 45,000 kilos of high explosive and incendiary bombs on the defenseless target. Von Richthofen noted exultantly in his diary: "Guernica has been literally razed to the ground. Bomb craters can be seen in the streets. Simply wonderful!"

Those on the ground found the situation less wonderful. Three-quarters of the buildings in the town were destroyed. Around 1,600 people were said to have been killed, though this figure was later claimed to be an exaggeration. Noel Monks, a British journalist covering the war for the Daily Express newspaper, arrived just after the attack and wrote: "I was the first correspondent to reach Guernica and was immediately pressed into service by some Basque soldiers collecting charred bodies. Some of the soldiers were sobbing like children. There were smoke and flames and grit, and the smell of burning human flesh was nauseating."

Many other journalists arrived in the devastated town and, unlike most of the massacres during the Spanish Civil War, the bombing of Guernica was reported around the world. International outrage was so great that Franco and the Condor Legion initially denied that the bombing had taken place at all, claiming that the destruction of Guernica was carried out by retreating Republican troops.

Guernica became a byword for the deliberate targeting of civilians during the civil war. There is no doubt that this was a terrible action, but it was merely one of many massacres carried out during this brutal war. Terror became a weapon used by both sides. Before the Spanish Civil War, the deliberate targeting of civilians in wartime was relatively uncommon. After 1939, this became an element of almost every war which followed.

Chapter Seven

The Nationalists Grow Stronger

"In modern war you will die like a dog for no good reason."

—Ernest Hemingway

By the middle of 1937, the Nationalists had become completely united under the command of General Franco. General Emilio Mola, who had commanded the Army of the North, was killed in an air crash on June 3. There were suspicions that Franco was nervous of the popularity of Mola and decided to have his rival killed. No evidence has ever been uncovered to support this contention, but with this accident happening just six months after the death of Franco's other main potential rival, General Sanjurjo, in an air crash, many senior Nationalists must have become nervous fliers at this time. Still, the death of Mola left the Nationalist side completely united under General Franco.

In contrast, the Republicans seemed to be tearing themselves apart. After almost one year of war, Stalin was even more determined to ensure that only communists loyal to the Soviet Union remained in the Popular Front. This meant a new round of purges amongst Republicans. NKVD agents and hit squads were sent to murder anyone whose loyalty was suspect and especially those who were followers of Trotsky.

Andrés Nin had been a founding member of the Spanish Communist Party (PCE), but he had also spent time in Russia where he had opposed Stalin's rise to power and spent time as Trotsky's secretary. When he returned to Spain, he founded the Marxist but anti-Stalinist POUM. Nin was charismatic, intelligent, and a focal point for members of the left wing in Spain who were nervous about the brutality of Stalin's regime. In mid-June 1937, the Popular Front government, under pressure from the PCE (who were themselves under pressure from Moscow) declared POUM illegal. Nin was arrested, brutally tortured, and executed by members of the NKVD. Many leaders and supporters of the POUM were also arrested and executed or forced to flee Spain; one of these was the English writer George Orwell, who had been fighting as a volunteer in a POUM militia unit in Catalonia.

At the same time, the Nationalists were growing stronger. Supplies of weapons and ammunition from Germany, Italy, and Portugal were flowing into Nationalist Spain, and military operations were stepped up.

In the Basque area of northern Spain, the Republicans had been forced back to the city of Bilbao, and on June 11, a Nationalist Army attacked the city supported by bombing attacks by the aircraft of the Condor Legion. On June 18, the last of the Republican defenders left the city, and it was occupied the following day. Around 200,000 civilians fled, and many made their way to the coast in the hope of reaching France by boat. Many of these small boats were destroyed by units of the Nationalist navy. The capture of the iron ore mines and steel factories of the Basque region were important to Franco. Not only did this assure the Nationalists a supply of steel, but the output from many of the ore mines had been promised to Germany in exchange for their supply of aircraft and tanks.

In July, the Republicans launched an attack intended to relieve the siege of Madrid. Like many Republican actions during this war, the attack on Brunete, 25 kilometers west of Madrid, was carried out with enthusiasm and great courage but poor organization. The attack involved around 80,000 men from four International Brigades supported by Russian T-26 tanks and I-16 aircraft. However, the troops were poorly equipped; many were using First World War weapons, and there was a serious shortage of ammunition.

In part, the attack was undertaken for political reasons to satisfy Russian advisors who were reporting back to Stalin that the Republican Army seemed unwilling to commit to a major attack—the Russians had been calling for an attack on Brunete since April. Stalin was wary of sending more Russian equipment and troops to Spain unless he felt that the Republicans had a realistic chance of winning the war. The attack on Brunete was an opportunity for them to demonstrate that they could achieve military victory.

On July 8, the Republican attack began. For eight days, their troops fought across difficult terrain and in extreme heat. By July 16, they had achieved many of their objectives but at a terrible cost. Although Nationalist units were sometimes outnumbered by ten to one, many fought with determination and great bravery. As a result, several Republican units had suffered 40% casualties. Some units of the International Brigades even reported losses approaching 80%. Republican troops were exhausted and critically short of food, water, medical supplies, and ammunition.

On July 18, the Nationalists mounted a massive counterattack with reserves diverted from the fighting near Bilbao. By July 25, Brunete had been re-taken, and the Republicans were back virtually to where they had started. They had lost some of their best troops and suffered approximately 23,000 casualties. They had also been forced to abandon large quantities of equipment which they could not afford to sacrifice. Morale, even in the elite International Brigades, was very low on the Republican side following this battle. The Nationalists also suffered very high casualties—estimates suggest that they lost around 17,000 men in just over two weeks of fighting around Brunete. However, the siege of Madrid continued, and the battles around Brunete were seen as a victory for the Nationalists.

The attack on Brunete was the largest Republican offensive of the civil war to date, and it had been intended to show Stalin and the world that they were capable of achieving a significant military victory. Instead, after some early success, the offensive was a catastrophe for the Republicans which demonstrated the precise opposite.

After Brunete, Stalin had major doubts about whether the Republican cause was worth supporting. Supplies of Russian tanks, aircraft, and guns rapidly dwindled to almost nothing after July 1937. Russian diplomatic missions to Spain were cut back, and many Russian pilots and tanks crews were recalled.

The Republican offensive at Brunete wasn't the end of the Spanish Civil War, but after this battle it was obvious to most people that the Republicans could not achieve victory on the battlefield. Even before the battle of Brunete, many outside observers believed that the Nationalists were likely to win the civil war. After Brunete, this seemed virtually certain—the only question was how long it would take.

Chapter Eight

Triumph in the North

"All the war propaganda, all the screaming and lies and hatred, comes invariably from people who are not fighting."

—George Orwell, *Homage to Catalonia* (1938)

In the region of Aragon in northeastern Spain, the Republicans continued their efforts to eradicate the influence of anarchist groups. Aragon was ruled during the early stages of the civil war by the Regional Defence Council of Aragon (RDCA), a group that was dominated by the anarchist CNT. Under the control of the RDCA, Aragon became an anarchist state within Republican Spain with widespread collective ownership of farms and businesses and suppression of the Catholic Church.

But on August 10, 1937, Prime Minister Negrín issued a decree dissolving the RDCA. Republican military units were dispatched to Aragon, the president of the RDCA and many of its members and supporters were arrested, and a number were executed. Newspapers controlled by the Popular Front—which by this time meant controlled by the communists—crowed: "The Popular Front Government has made a truly triumphant entry into Aragon. The jubilant peasants, filled with expectation, welcomed it. An era of hateful tragedy has assuredly passed."

The truth was that many of the people of Aragon had welcomed the RDCA and the revolutionary changes it brought to their lives. Many were resentful of the dissolution of the group and the imposition of central rule by the government. To many people, it seemed that Negrín and the communist-dominated cabinet of the Popular Front had abandoned the socialist and liberal ideals it had once stood for and instead sought to impose communist rule over all of Republican Spain. At a time when the military situation looked grave for the Republicans, they once again appeared to be wasting men and resources on internal squabbles.

The loss of Bilbao to the Nationalists in June had been a major blow to the Republican Army of the North, but worse was to follow. In mid-August, Nationalist armies under the command of General Fidel Davila launched an attack on the Republican-held province of Santander. They were opposed by large numbers of Republican troops, but Republican morale was poor, and their units suffered from a lack of modern weapons and ammunition. The ensuing series of battles were brief and bitter, and on August 26, the Nationalists occupied the city of Santander.

Losses to the Republicans were very serious; a total of 60,000 men were killed, wounded, or captured. Seventeen thousand Republican troops were captured when the city of Santander fell, and many of these were immediately executed. The Republican Army of the North never recovered from this loss of men or from the loss of their equipment, and by the end of August 1937, the city of Gijon was the only remaining Republican stronghold on the northern coast of Spain.

The Popular Front responded to this latest military setback by creating a new secret police force, the Servicio de Información Militar (SIM) to further attack non-communist elements of the Popular Front. The SIM, which included large numbers of Russian advisers, became notorious for its use of torture and extra-legal execution in its attempts to eradicate anarchist and non-Stalinist Marxist groups. Two SIM secret prisons were established in Madrid and Barcelona, and it has been estimated that this group killed as many as one thousand Republicans during the civil war. Once again, the Popular Front seemed more concerned about the suppression of non-Stalinist Republicans than with fighting the Nationalists.

On August 28, the Vatican formally recognized Franco's regime. This was an important step towards the legitimization of the Nationalist cause and a recognition that it might soon be ruling all of Spain. At the end of August, the Republican Army of the East launched a counter-attack in Aragon, aiming to recapture the cities of Saragossa, Huesca, and Teruel. By the end of September, this Republican offensive had ground to a halt without achieving any of its objectives but having suffered large numbers of casualties.

At the beginning of September, the Nationalists attacked the city of Gijon through the mountains of Leon.

The battle was a tough one for both sides, but by October 21, Nationalist forces occupied the city. The whole of the northern coast of Spain was now in Nationalist hands, and the Republican Army of the North was suffering from low morale due to a lack of supplies and heavy casualties in August and September. By the end of October, the civil war was all but over in northern Spain with the Nationalists triumphant.

On November 31, 1937, the Republican government relocated once more, this time from Valencia to Barcelona. The Nationalist success in the north threatened Valencia, and it was clear that Catalonia was one of the last safe Republican areas in Spain.

Chapter Nine

The Republicans Fight Back

"The gift of Teruel at Christmas had become for the Republicans no more than a poisoned toy: it was meant to be the victory that would change the war; it was instead the seal of defeat."

—Laurie Lee

As 1937 drew to an end, it was clear that the year had been a military disaster for the Republicans. Their assault on Brunete had not achieved its objectives and had cost massive casualties, and the Nationalists now controlled all of northern Spain. Indalecio Prieto had been appointed Minister of War for the Popular Front in May 1937, and there had been ferocious criticism of his leadership during the year. It was becoming difficult to find supplies for Republican troops; the now limited Russian aid arriving by sea was subject to attacks by Italian submarines, and the border with France was closed. Prieto embarked on an extensive reorganization of the Republican armies in the autumn of 1937, and what he and the Popular Front needed was a decisive Republican military victory to prove to the world that their cause was not lost.

The location chosen for this battle was the city of Teruel in the province of Aragon in eastern Spain.

Following Nationalist advances in September and October, Teruel was on a narrow salient of Nationalist land surrounded on three sides by Republican forces. The city is known for the severity of its winters—it lies more than 3,000 feet above sea level and very often has the lowest temperatures in the whole of Spain. The winter of 1937-1938 was proving to be the worst for 20 years.

The Republicans managed to muster two armies totaling around 100,000 men for the attack on Teruel. The defending Nationalist forces numbered under 10,000. The attack on the city began on December 15 as snow began to fall. The fighting was intense, and the extreme cold made survival unlikely for the wounded. By Christmas Day, the few remaining Nationalist defenders were holding out in a cluster of buildings at the southern end of the city. Republican radio announced that the city had been captured, but this proved to be premature. On December 29, a Nationalist counter-attack began, and by December 31, they had entered the outskirts of town. Then the weather took its toll. A four-day blizzard brought more than four feet of snow and temperatures fell to -20°C. The Nationalist troops had little winter clothing or equipment and their counter-attack stalled.

On January 8, the last of the original Nationalist defenders of Teruel finally surrendered including the commander, Colonel Domingo Rey d'Harcourt, and the bishop of Teruel. D'Harcourt, the bishop, and 41 other captured Nationalist soldiers were promptly executed by the Republicans.

By January 17, 1938, the weather had improved, and the Nationalists mounted a large-scale attack to retake Teruel with the support of the aircraft of the Condor Legion. The attack progressed slowly until February 7 when a Nationalist cavalry attack (the last large-scale cavalry action in the history of warfare) broke through Republican defenses north of Teruel. The final assault on the city began on February 18, and by February 22, Teruel was back in Nationalist hands.

Thousands of Republican troops were captured, and tons of essential supplies fell into Nationalist hands. The Nationalist forces occupying the city found more than 10,000 Republican corpses. The two-month battle cost over 140,000 casualties in total and massive air battles over the city led to significant losses of aircraft and pilots. For the Republicans, these losses were irreplaceable. With their supplies of new equipment severely curtailed by the Nationalist occupation of Spain's northern coast, the aircraft, tanks, and weapons they lost at Teruel were never replaced.

But the loss to Republican morale was even more serious. The Republicans had needed a decisive victory to persuade their supporters around the world that there were capable of winning the war. Instead, Teruel was the point at which the defeat of the Republicans seemed inevitable.

Teruel also opened the way for the Nationalists to the Mediterranean coast. If they could reach the coast, they could split the remaining Republican part of Spain in two, making their situation even more desperate.

Chapter Ten

The End of the War

"I have the most evil memories of Spain, but I have very few bad memories of Spaniards."

—George Orwell, *Homage to Catalonia* (1938)

On March 7, 1938, Nationalist forces drove south from the Teruel salient. Their objective was the Mediterranean coast and an attempt to split the remaining Republican-held territory in two. The Republican defenders were numerous but inexperienced, and some lacked even rifles and ammunition. The fighting was bitter, but the Nationalist advance was unstoppable. There were desertions and mutiny amongst Republican forces. The response was arbitrary executions, with some officers being shot in front of their men. None of this made any difference, and on April 15, Nationalist forces reached the town of Vinaros on the Mediterranean coast. Republican Spain was split into two separate zones with Barcelona in the east and Madrid and Valencia in the west.

On May 1, Popular Front Prime Minister Negrín proposed peace terms to the Nationalists, a tacit admission that the war was lost. Franco's response was unequivocal: he would accept nothing but the unconditional surrender of all Republican forces.

However, the election of a left-wing leader, Leon Blum, in France led to the re-opening of the border with Spain, and the Republicans were finally able to receive the supplies they desperately needed. They also introduced conscription of men as young as 16 (the "baby-bottle call-up") and applied pressure to Nationalist prisoners of war to join the Republican army. By the evening of July 24, the Republicans had somehow managed to scrape together sufficient troops to mount an attack over the Ebro River near the town of Fayón to begin the last, biggest, and bloodiest battle of the Spanish Civil War.

For five months the Republicans threw everything they had into the attack. Initially they took ground, but the cost in men, supplies, and equipment was too great. By the middle of November 1938, the last Republican troops had retreated back over their starting point on the Ebro River. Total casualties were over 100,000 for both sides. The Nationalists were able to replace their losses, but the Republicans could not. The battles on the Ebro River marked the end of the Republican Army as an effective fighting force.

In January 1939, Nationalist forces captured Barcelona, and the Popular Front government was forced to relocate once more, this time to the small city of Figueres in Catalonia. On February 4, Popular Front President Manuel Azaña fled over the border into France. On March 27, after three years of siege, Nationalist troops occupied Madrid. On March 30, Nationalists occupied the last Republican stronghold of Valencia. Finally, on April

1, 1939, General Franco made a formal announcement that the Spanish Civil War was over.

The Spanish Civil War is thought to have directly caused the deaths of around half a million people. Two hundred thousand were troops killed in combat; the others were civilians. In the years following the official end of the war, Nationalist oppression continued as small pockets of Republican fighters held out in some areas. The roots of terrorist groups like ETA—the Basque Separatist organization which assassinated Luis Carrero Blanco in 1973, the man widely predicted to be Franco's successor—can be traced directly to Republican groups which emerged during the civil war. The transfer of a large proportion of the Spanish gold reserve to Russia during the war plus the costs of rebuilding meant poverty for many Spanish people for a number of years, and the rule of Franco continued to be ruthless and oppressive. Censorship of the press remained until 1975.

The Spanish Civil War brought political stability to Spain, but at a terrible cost. For many Spanish people, the recent violent response to Catalan separatists has revived memories of the civil war, and these—even though they are seldom discussed—are rarely far below the surface of Spanish society.

Conclusion

When the Spanish Civil War began in July 1936, few people believed that the rebel Nationalists had any chance of acquiring power. After all, they were taking on an established and well-supported government with all the resources of the Spanish state available to it. When the fighting began, it became clear that the situation was more complex than it appeared.

The support of Nazi Germany and Fascist Italy for the Nationalists proved to be very significant. Had it not been for the German aircraft used to transport General Franco and the troops of the Army of Morocco to Spain, the general's revolt might well have been a failure from the start. The continuing support of these countries gave Franco a distinct advantage throughout the war when his Republican enemies often struggled to find the equipment and ammunition necessary to continue fighting.

The character of Francisco Franco also proved to be very significant. General Franco was ruthless but also intelligent and an able military leader. His drive and focus pulled the Nationalist side together while the Republicans lacked a single strong leader and often seemed more interested in fighting amongst themselves than fighting the Nationalists.

After the civil war, Franco proved to be adept at leading Spain. A little more than one year after the end of fighting in Spain, Hitler's troops invaded Poland, and World War II began. Benito Mussolini quickly drew Italy into the war, and both dictators confidently assumed that Franco would repay their support during the Spanish Civil War by entering World War II on the Axis side. Instead, the wily Franco set so many conditions on Spain joining the war that the country actually stayed neutral. Hitler once said that he would rather visit a dentist to have several teeth removed than to negotiate with General Franco.

Francisco Franco continued to rule Spain until his death in November 1975 at the age of 83. His rule was authoritarian and anti-communist, and democracy did not return to Spain until after his death. Immediately after World War II, Spain maintained a separation from the rest of Europe. Franco felt that he had little in common with the countries which had defeated his allies, Germany and Italy. It wasn't until after his death that Spain became fully integrated into Europe when it joined the EU in 1986.

The Spanish Civil War was important not just as a precursor to World War II, but because it graphically showed that a right-wing, militaristic regime could not only come to power through armed insurrection in Europe, it could remain in power until the death of its leader. Adolf Hitler ruled Germany for just 11 years. Mussolini was the undisputed leader of Italy for 20 years. But in Spain, Francisco Franco ruled for almost 40 years. When people think of fascist leaders of the 1930s, it is Hitler and Mussolini that they usually consider. Yet, thanks to the Spanish Civil War, Francisco Franco ruled Spain long after his two contemporaries were dead.